One day Kevin and Lotty go to play in the lane. They run until they come to a gate.

Kevin and Lotty creep under the gate. Kevin takes Lotty along a little path to some big rocks.

Kevin and Lotty play on the rocks. They play a jumping game. It makes them hot.

They sit on the grass in the shade of the big rocks. Then Kevin sees a cave in the rocks.

Kevin takes Lotty into the cave. It is cool in the cave. The two dogs go to sleep.

It is late in the day when Lotty wakes up. She feels afraid. She shakes Kevin to wake him up.

"Hiss ... sss." Oh no! There is a snake in the cave. "Hiss ... sss." Lotty shakes Kevin again. He wakes up. He is afraid too.

Kevin and Lotty must be brave. They creep past the snake and run out of the cave as fast as they can.

They run back to the gate and creep under it. They run back along the lane to the kennel.

Soon they are safe in the kennel with Wellington. They tell him the tale of the snake in the cave. "You have been very brave," he says.

"a-e"

tale	lane
gate	game
cave	snake
makes	safe
shakes	shade
wakes	late
takes	brave

High Frequency Words

day and go to play in the
are they come a big it on of
sees is dogs up she no he
can you

one little some them then two
when him there again too be
out as back with have been
very must jumping makes takes